T0283268

There were small dragons in his body, trying to eat their way out. That's what it felt like, anyway.

In a small village in Ghana, Africa, Karim Fusheni and six members of his family were in agonizing pain.

The Diagnosis

The whole family was itching and blistering. They had burning sores.

Mr. Kofi, a local health-care worker, recognized the symptoms immediately. The family was suffering from terrible parasites that Kofi had hoped were gone from Ghana for good—guinea worms.

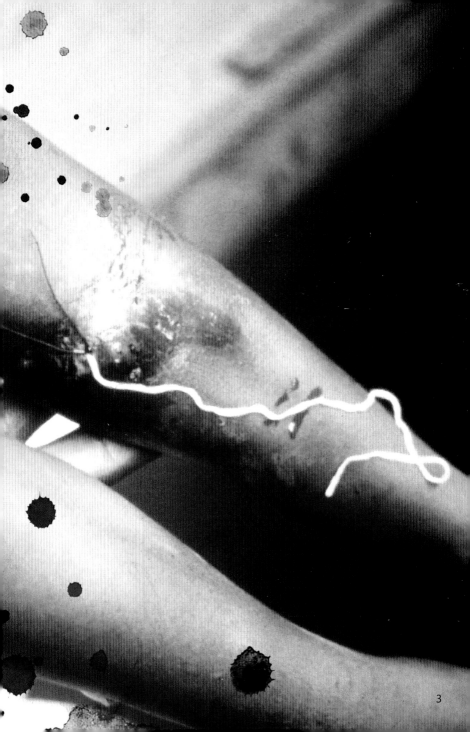

Detective Work

Kofi acted fast. He called in a medical team to help remove the worms.

Now Kofi had to find out where the worms had come from. How had the Fushenis become infected? And what about other villagers—were they at risk?

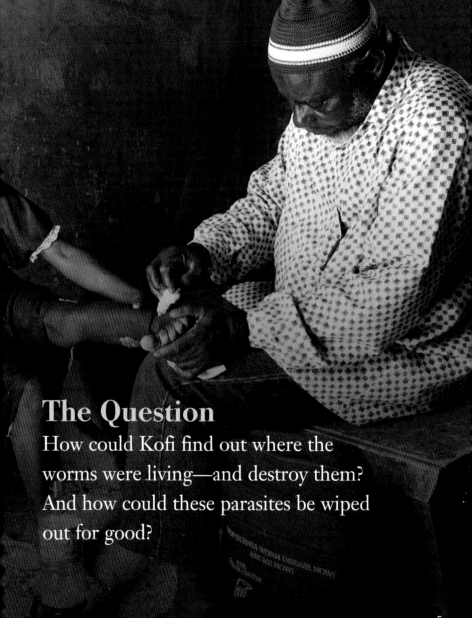

The Question

How could Kofi find out where the worms were living—and destroy them? And how could these parasites be wiped out for good?

PREVIEW PHOTOS

PAGE 1: A man in Niger, Africa, is treated for a guinea worm in his back.

PAGES 2-3: A worm is partially extracted from a patient's leg.

PAGES 4-5: A young girl in Ghana is treated for guinea worm by a health-care worker.

Cover design: Maria Bergós, Book&Look **Interior design:** Red Herring Design/NYC

Photo Credits ©: cover top: Robin Loznak/ZUMAPRESS.com/Alamy Images; cover bottom: E. Staub/The Carter Center; 1: Karen Kasmauski/National Geographic Creative; 2-3: Clinical Photography, Central Manchester University Hospitals NHS Foundation Trust, UK/Science Source; 4-5: L. Gubb/The Carter Center; 8: John Bazemore/AP Images; 10: L. Gubb/The Carter Center; 13: Sean Sprague/Alamy Images; 14: Airelle-Joubert/Science Source; 15: E. Staub/The Carter Center; 16-17 background: The Carter Center; 16 left: baona/Getty Images; 16 right: M. I. Walker/Science Source; 17 bottom: The Carter Center; 18: J. Albertson/The Carter Center; 20: E. Staub/The Carter Center; 23: Karen Kasmauski; 24-25: L. Gubb/The Carter Center; 26: The Carter Center; 28: Clinical Photography, Central Manchester University Hospitals NHS Foundation Trust, UK/Science Source; 30 top:. Gubb/The Carter Center; 30 bottom: The Carter Center; 31: The Carter Center; 32: E. Staub/The Carter Center; 34: E. Staub/The Carter Center; 36: The Carter Center; 37: Lester V. Bergman/Getty Images; 38: The Carter Center; 40 top: Jennie Hart/Alamy Images; 40 bottom left: Jorge Rimblas/Getty Images; 40 bottom right: J. Albertson/The Carter Center; 41 top left: skegbydave/Getty Images; 41 bottom: Seth Lazer/Alamy Images; 42 top: Dr. Fred Hossler/Visuals Unlimited; 42 center top: CDC/Science Source; 42, center bottom: Dr. Arthur Siegelman/Visuals Unlimited; 42 bottom left: John Bazemore/AP Images; 42 bottom right: Lester V. Bergman/Getty Images; 43: Dr. Fred Hossler/Visuals Unlimited; 44-45: J. Albertson/The Carter Center.

All other photos © Shutterstock.

Library of Congress Cataloging-in-Publication Data
Names: Tilden, Thomasine E. Lewis, 1958- author.
Title: Dangerous worms : parasites plague a village / Thomasine E. Lewis Tilden.
Description: [New edition] | New York : Children's Press/Scholastic Inc., 2020.
| Series: Xbooks | Originally published: New York : Scholastic, ©2012.
| Audience: Ages 8-10. | Audience: Grades 4-6. | Summary: "Book introduces the reader
to dangerous worms"-- Provided by publisher. Identifiers: LCCN 2020008047 | ISBN 9780531132302
(library binding) | ISBN 9780531132951 (paperback) Subjects: LCSH: Guinea worm--Juvenile literature.
| Dracunculiasis--Ghana--Juvenile literature. | Parasites--Juvenile literature.
Classification: LCC QL757 .T55 2020 | DDC 592/.3--dc23
LC record available at https://lccn.loc.gov/2020008047

No part of this publication may be reproduced in whole or in part, or stored in a retrieval system,
or transmitted in any form or by any means, electronic, mechanical, photocopying, recording, or otherwise,
without written permission of the publisher. For information regarding permission, write to Scholastic Inc.,
Attention: Permissions Department, Scholastic Inc., 557 Broadway, New York, NY 10012.

© 2021, 2012, 2008 Scholastic Inc.

All rights reserved. Published by Scholastic Inc.

Printed in Johor Bahru, Malaysia   108

1 2 3 4 5 6 7 8 9 10 R 30 29 28 27 26 25 24 23 22 21

SCHOLASTIC, XBOOKS, and associated logos are trademarks and/or registered trademarks of Scholastic Inc.

Scholastic Inc., 557 Broadway, New York, NY 10012.

DANGEROUS
WORMS

Parasites Plague a Village

THOMASINE E. LEWIS TILDEN

GUINEA WORMS are
parasites that grow
inside the human body.

TABLE OF CONTENTS

1

Return of the Worms!

A parasite makes a family in Ghana sick.

Every day a health-care worker named Mr. Kofi sets off to examine people in villages near his home. Kofi lives in Ghana, a country on the west coast of Africa. His job is to help control the guinea worm problem there. He keeps an eye out for people with symptoms of guinea worm disease.

And he hopes he doesn't find any.

Guinea worms are parasites that are found in

parts of Asia and Africa. A parasite is a tiny life-form that infects a host animal. It depends on its host for food and other basic needs. Fleas and ticks are types of parasites. They attach themselves to animals and feed on their blood. Unfortunately, the guinea worm's favorite host is the human body!

People get guinea worm disease by drinking water that's infested with water fleas. The fleas carry guinea worm larvae—the young form of the worm. The larvae escape from the infected person's stomach and burrow into their intestines.

Once the guinea worms are fully grown, they start to make their way out of the body. How do they get out? Through the skin! That's when things get really painful.

People infected with guinea worms suffer terrible pain, itching, and burning as the worms try to exit their bodies. The disease is so painful that its medical name is dracunculiasis. That means "pain caused by little dragons." And if the worms aren't removed properly, they can cause serious infections.

THESE TWO BOYS live in a small village in Ghana. In that country, 60 percent of guinea worm disease cases occurred in children.

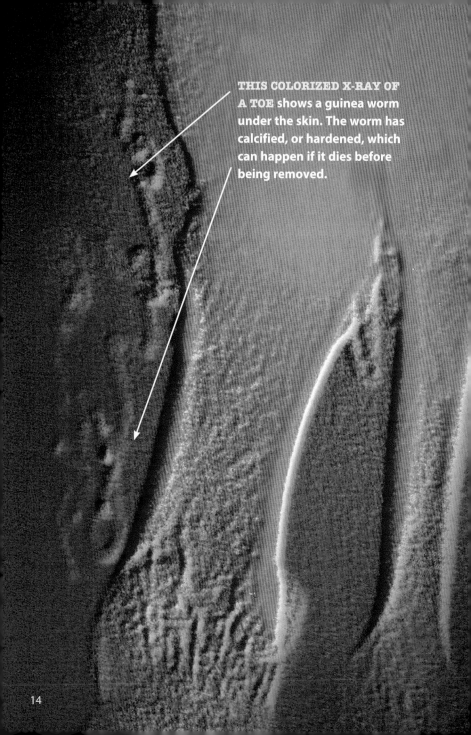

THIS COLORIZED X-RAY OF A TOE shows a guinea worm under the skin. The worm has calcified, or hardened, which can happen if it dies before being removed.

A Family in Trouble

In March 2006, Kofi arrived at the home of the Fusheni family. Seven of the 10 family members were seriously ill. The grandmother's feet were swollen with blisters. She couldn't collect firewood. The parents were too weak to farm the fields. The two young children itched terribly. And the two older boys had open wounds on their legs. They had trouble walking, and they could not go to school.

Kofi knew right away that the Fushenis were infected with guinea worms. But where had the worms come from? And why weren't any other villagers sick?

A VOLUNTEER IN NIGERIA extracts a guinea worm from a man's leg. Nigeria is another country in West Africa.

Unwelcome Guests

Follow the guinea worms on their tour of destruction—through your body!

1. You drink dirty water that contains tiny animals called water fleas. The water fleas are infected with guinea worm larvae—the young form of the worm.

2. The water fleas die in your stomach. The guinea worm larvae burrow into the walls of your intestines.

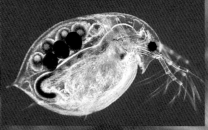

Water flea

6. Water fleas eat the larvae, and the cycle begins again. Meanwhile, back inside your body, the adult worms die. If they're not removed, they cause a serious infection. They can harden and cause terrible pain in the muscles and joints.

3. Over the next nine to 12 months, several things happen:

• The larvae grow into adult worms.

• The male and female worms mate, and the males die.

• The female worms travel through your body—usually to your feet or legs.

All the while, the females grow. They can get as wide as spaghetti noodles and as long as four feet (1.2 meters)!

4. About one year after you become infected, the female guinea worms wriggle to the surface of your skin. This causes the skin to blister.

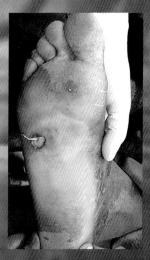

5. When you soak your blisters in water, the worms feel the change in temperature. They poke about one inch (2.5 centimeters) out of the wound and release millions of larvae. Then the worms shrink back into your body.

A LOCAL VOLUNTEER in the African country of Sudan educates kids about guinea worm prevention.

2

Kofi on the Case

He's a health-care worker and a guinea worm detective.

An outbreak of guinea worm disease in a small village is a serious matter. People live close together. They share many of the same resources. That means other people in the Fushenis' village were at risk of getting guinea worms, too.

Kofi had his work cut out for him. And he needed help. First he called a medical team to tend to the Fusheni family. Their worms had to be removed.

A WOMAN IN NIGERIA, AFRICA, draws water from a local pond. To make it safe to drink, the water must be filtered to remove the fleas that carry guinea worms.

The process is slow, complicated, and painful.

Next, Kofi turned his attention to some detective work.

Kofi had figured out the *what*: guinea worm disease. And he knew *when* the Fushenis had become infected, too. The worms were causing blisters. That meant the worms had been growing for nine to 12 months. About one year before, the Fushenis must have drunk contaminated water.

Source of Contamination

But *where* had the water come from? There were three possibilities. The Fushenis could have been infected from a water source that the entire village shared. Or they could have traveled outside the area and drunk contaminated water. Or perhaps they had a private water source that was contaminated.

Kofi knew that the first possibility was not likely. No one else in the village had become infected with guinea worms in the past year. If the community water source were contaminated, other people in the village would be infected.

Kofi asked the Fushenis whether they had traveled during the last year. None of them had left the village. Next, Kofi asked whether they had a private water source. At first he was told no. But Kofi doubted the answer. He kept repeating the question. And he explained how important the information was.

A Hidden Pond

Finally, the grandmother admitted that they had a small pond on the farm. She said that the children liked to swim there. They also drank from the pond sometimes.

Kofi asked the children about the pond. One of the boys remembered that a cousin had visited a year earlier. The cousin had a sore on his leg.

Kofi had solved the mystery. The cousin probably had guinea worms. When he swam in the pond, the worms released their larvae.

Luckily, the Fushenis had not used the community water source in the last year. The rest of the village was safe from infection.

Now it was time to treat the Fusheni family.

WATER HOLES, like this one in the West African country of Mali, might be the only source for washing and drinking water during very dry periods.

Slaying the Dragon Worm

The Carter Center leads the fight to wipe out the guinea worm.

Who they are: The Carter Center was founded in 1982 by former U.S. president Jimmy Carter and his wife, Rosalynn.

Their mission: In 1986, the center began a program to eradicate—wipe out— guinea worm disease. The Carter Center continues to work to eradicate guinea worm in the African countries of South Sudan, Mali, Chad, Ethiopia, and Angola.

Drinking filters: The Carter Center workers give people in infected areas drinking straws with filters, called pipe filters. They filter out the water fleas that might be infected with guinea worms.

Clean water: The workers dig wells to reach clean water. They treat ponds with a chemical that kills the water fleas. And they teach people with guinea worm sores not to bathe in water that people drink from.

FORMER U.S. PRESIDENT Jimmy Carter speaks to a group of children in Ghana.

Victory in sight: In 1986, there were about 3.5 million cases of the disease. In 2009, there were just 3,190 cases. By 2018, the cases of Guinea worm had been reduced by 99.99 percent. There were only 28 cases that year.

Another disease The Carter Center is fighting: River blindness is also caused by a parasitic worm. Almost 18 million people have been infected. About 270,000 of them have gone blind.

Honors: In 2006, The Carter Center received the Gates Award for Global Health for fighting diseases that harm the world's poorest people.

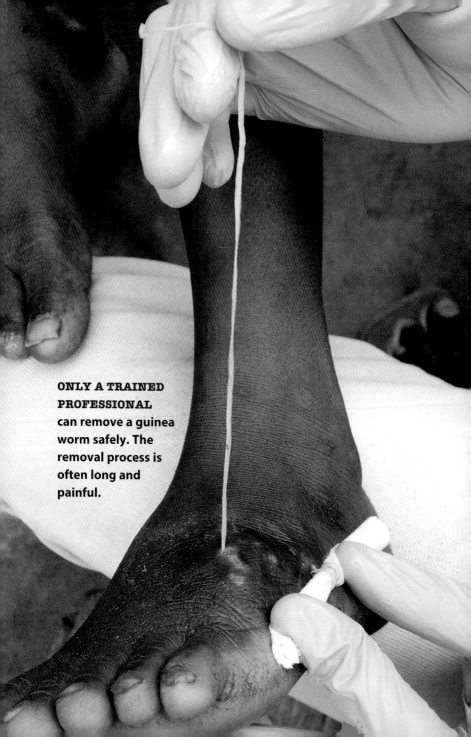

ONLY A TRAINED PROFESSIONAL can remove a guinea worm safely. The removal process is often long and painful.

3

Worm on a Stick

There's only one way to get rid of guinea worms. And it isn't pretty.

A team of health-care workers had arrived to help Kofi. Together they began to carefully remove the worms that were tormenting the Fusheni family. The process takes time and a lot of patience.

Kofi began by treating the oldest boy, Karim. Two worms were already hanging out of his sores. Kofi carefully cleaned the area around the wounds.

Then he pulled gently on the end of a worm.

Little by little, the worm began to come out. But Kofi knew not to force it. Guinea worms stretch like rubber bands. They will break if they're pulled too hard. That would cause most of the worm to die and shrink back into the body. The dead worm would cause pain and swelling and could lead to a dangerous infection.

A GUINEA WORM is slowly wound onto a stick. The stick is then taped to the patient's skin. Every few days, the worm is wound around the stick a little more, until the worm comes all the way out.

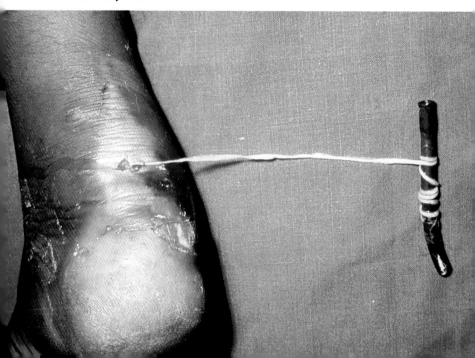

Tying Up the Worm

Eventually Kofi believed that he had pulled the worm out as much as he should. So he took a tiny piece of a stick from a tree. He wrapped the exposed part of the worm around the stick over and over. Then he taped the stick to Karim's leg so the worm would not unwind.

Kofi did the same thing with Karim's other worm. Then Kofi bandaged the wounds to keep them clean and hold the worms in place. He promised to return in two days.

While the Fushenis waited, water fleas infected with guinea worm larvae still swam in their pond. It was time to get rid of the fleas before the worms could find another host.

Armed for a Fight

Here are some frequently asked questions about treating guinea worm disease.

THE CARTER CENTER enlists local volunteers to help spread the word about preventing guinea worm disease.

Why are guinea worms so hard to treat?

No medication can kill the worm once it is inside of you. And there is no medication that prevents you from getting the worm.

Can the worm be coaxed out?

You can fool the worm by getting a large bucket of water and putting the infected body part in it. This brings the worm out to release its larvae. The water also helps lubricate the worm, making it easier to pull out.

A VOLUNTEER IN GHANA shows children how to use pipe filters to drink water.

What happens once the worm is wound around a stick?

The part on the stick begins to dry. That makes it harder for the worm to pull itself back into the body.

What happens if the worm isn't removed?

Shortly after the worm releases its larvae, it dies. If it's not removed, it causes serious infections. Some worms that never reach the skin's surface turn hard. It is as if they turn into sticks inside the body.

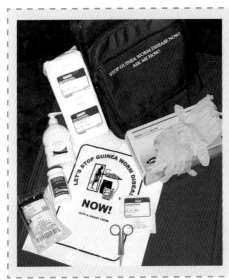

Gloves: worn to protect health-care workers and patients from each other's germs

Gauze packets: cloth and tape to cover wounds

Ointment: to place on wounds to prevent additional infection

Notebook: for the volunteer to record all guinea worm activity

Small wooden sticks: used to wrap the worms around

GUINEA WORM KITS like this one are distributed by The Carter Center to village-based volunteer health-care workers in countries with guinea worm disease. Each kit gives volunteers the tools they need to care for 10 people who suffer from guinea worm disease.

A WOMAN USES A PIPE FILTER to drink from a pond in Ghana. A screen in the pipe filters out the water fleas that carry guinea worms.

4

Spreading the Word

A simple tool—and an important message—help combat guinea worm disease.

Every two days, health-care workers returned to treat the Fusheni family. Each time, they carefully worked on removing the worms. Slowly, they made progress.

In the meantime, Kofi visited the Fushenis' pond. He estimated how much water it contained. He carefully measured out the right amount of a larvicide called ABATE. This chemical kills the larvae of

A RED CROSS VOLUNTEER in Ghana shows how to strain drinking water through a fine-mesh cloth filter to remove water fleas.

guinea worms, mosquitoes, and other parasites. Then Kofi poured the larvicide into the pond. Within six hours, the guinea worms and water fleas in the pond were dead.

An End to the Agony

ABATE is just one of the weapons African countries are using against guinea worms. Many villages now have filters to strain fleas from their drinking water. Public-health workers also give pipe filters to children. Pipe filters are hard plastic straws with a screen at the bottom end. Children wear them around their necks so they can drink filtered water wherever they go.

Karim Fusheni might have been spared a lot of agony if he'd had a pipe filter. The worms had wrapped themselves around tendons and muscles in his legs. Simply taking a step caused terrible pain.

It took three weeks for Kofi to remove the first worm from Karim's leg. It was almost four feet (1.2 m) long.

Kofi and his team worked with the Fushenis for two months. In the end, the seven infected family members recovered. Between them, they had hosted a total of 26 worms.

Once Karim was well, he decided to help others learn from his experience. He traveled to other villages to tell people about guinea worms.

By 2011, there was good news. Ghana had been worm-free for one year. And by 2018, there were only 28 cases of Guinea worm around the world. That is a 99.99 percent reduction in the disease! **X**

CHILDREN IN GHANA read a picture book about guinea worm after being treated for the disease.

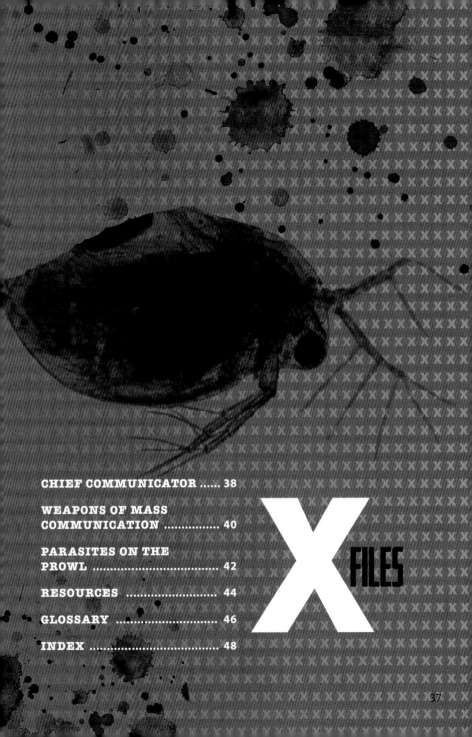

X FILES

Chief Communicator

Aryc Mosher spreads the word about guinea worm disease.

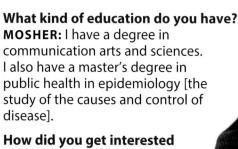

What kind of education do you have?
MOSHER: I have a degree in communication arts and sciences. I also have a master's degree in public health in epidemiology [the study of the causes and control of disease].

How did you get interested in public health?
MOSHER: I was always interested in developing messages to help change people. After college, I signed up with the Peace Corps. I went to Africa to work for three and a half years on AIDS and HIV prevention.

ARYC W. MOSHER was the assistant director for The Carter Center Guinea Worm Eradication Program from 2005 to 2007.

Years later, I ended up in Ghana working as an adviser to the National Guinea Worm Eradication Program.

What did you do in Ghana?

MOSHER: I developed proposals for the guinea worm program. I attended ceremonies and met with village chiefs. Sometimes villages did not want to have a chemical (ABATE) put into their water. They had heard that it would make them sick or sterile or kill the fish. So I'd go in with a team and talk to the chief and convince them it was safe.

What was the most memorable case you worked on?

MOSHER: A young boy, maybe 12 years old, who biked about 25 miles (40 kilometers) to our office to have his guinea worms treated. It was quite a physical act. Here was a young person wanting to get control of his situation and determined to do something about it.

Any suggestions for someone who wants to have a career in public health?

MOSHER: You can volunteer at hospitals or work for public-health campaigns—like the anti-smoking campaign, for example. Think of anything that helps people live healthier lives. In college, you can take classes in health communications and health promotions.

If you want to travel and get public-health experience overseas, go online and check out organizations like the Peace Corps or Project HOPE. There are lots of opportunities to see the world, gain experience in health issues, and make a difference in people's lives.

Weapons of Mass Communication

Here are some of the things that public-health workers use while getting the word out.

1

1 Family photos When foreign workers arrive in a village, one of the best ways to break the ice is to share family photos—especially of their kids or mothers. Photos help people get to know one another.

2 Cloth charts Workers travel from village to village to teach people about guinea worm disease. They carry cloth charts with illustrations showing how to use pipe filters. The cloth charts can be easily rolled up, carried, and stored.

2

3 Laptop computers, flash drives, and cell phones
When traveling, public-health workers need access to their home offices and to medical researchers around the globe. They rely on portable devices to keep connected.

4 Motorcycle
In rural areas, the quickest and easiest way to get around is by motorcycle.

5 Hat, sunglasses, sunscreen
Workers who travel near the equator need protection from the hot sun. Foreign workers also dress professionally as a sign of respect for their hosts.

Parasites on the Prowl

	Parasite	Host	How can you get it?	Where can you get it?
	Giardia lamblia	Humans	Swimming in a lake or stream and drinking the water	Anywhere there are lakes or streams
	Taenia solium (pork tapeworm)	Pigs	Eating undercooked pork infected with the parasite	Anywhere people eat pork
	Leishmania	Sand flies	Getting bitten by a sand fly	Deserts and jungles— mostly in India, Bangladesh, Nepal, Sudan, and Brazil
	Dracunculus medinensis (guinea worm)	Water fleas	Drinking water infected with the fleas	Countries in Asia and Africa

Guinea worms aren't the only parasites that can make people sick. Check out these fast facts about the guinea worm and other unwelcome guests.

Where does it live in humans?	What are the symptoms?	How is it diagnosed?	What is the treatment?
Intestines and stomach	Diarrhea, stomachache, bloating, weight loss	Examining stool samples	Medication
Small intestine, brain, eye tissue, and liver	In the brain, it causes seizures and lesions. In other areas it can cause sores.	Examining stool samples	Medication. Sometimes surgery is needed for eye or brain infections.
In the blood. It may travel to the mouth and nose.	Raised, pus-filled sores on the skin. Patients usually have fever and weight loss.	Testing the pus and blood, examining tissue samples, and checking for enlarged spleen and liver	Medication
First in the intestine. Then it usually travels to the legs and feet.	Itching and burning when the worm starts to come out of the skin	Seeing blisters where worms have created openings or seeing the worms emerge	Slowly twisting the worm around a stick until it is completely out of the body

43

RESOURCES

Here's a selection of books for more information about guinea worms and other parasites.

NONFICTION

Axelrod-Contrada, Joan. *Mini Mind Controllers: Fungi, Bacteria, and Other Tiny Zombie Makers (Real-Life Zombies).* North Mankato, Minnesota: Capstone, 2016.

Brown, Jordan D. *Micro Mania: A Really Close-Up Look at Bacteria, Bedbugs & the Zillions of Other Gross Little Creatures That Live In, On & All Around You!* Watertown, Massachusetts: Charlesbridge, 2009.

Cohn, Jessica. *Parasite Collector (Dirty and Dangerous Jobs).* Salt Lake City, Utah: Benchmark Books, 2010.

Davies, Nicola. *What's Eating You?: Parasites—The Inside Story (Animal Science).* Somerville, Massachusetts: Candlewick, 2009.

DiConsiglio, John. *There's a Fungus Among Us! True Stories of Killer Molds (24/7: Science Behind the Scenes: Medical Files).* New York: Franklin Watts, 2007.

Haelle, Tara. *Insects as Parasites.* Vero Beach, Florida: Rourke Educational Media, 2016.

Owen, Ruth. *Gross Body Invaders (Up Close and Gross: Microscopic Creatures).* New York: Bearport Publishing, 2011.

Quinlan, Susan. *The Case of the Monkeys That Fell from the Trees: And Other Mysteries in Tropical Nature.* Honesdale, Pennsylvania: Boyds Mills Press, 2010.

Ramen, Fred. *Sleeping Sickness and Other Parasitic Tropical Diseases (Epidemics).* New York: Rosen, 2002.

Tilden, Thomasine. *Belly-busting Worm Invasions! Parasites That Love Your Insides! (24/7: Science Behind the Scenes: Medical Files).* New York: Franklin Watts, 2007.

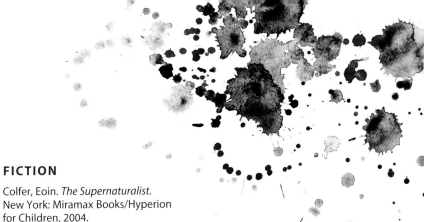

FICTION

Colfer, Eoin. *The Supernaturalist.*
New York: Miramax Books/Hyperion
for Children, 2004.

Holm, Jennifer L. *Squish #3: The
Power of the Parasite.* New York:
Random House, 2012.

Iwaaki, Hitoshi. *Parasyte 1.*
New York: Ballantine, 2011.

CHILDREN with
pipe filters

GLOSSARY

agonizing (AG-uh-nize-ing) *adjective* extremely painful

calcify (KAL-sih-fye) *verb* to harden because of deposits of the mineral calcium

contaminated (kuhn-TAM-uh-nay-tid) *adjective* made dirty by something harmful

diagnosis (dye-uhg-NOH-sis) *noun* the identification of a condition or disease

dracunculiasis (dra-kun-kuh-LYE-uh-sis) *noun* an infection caused by drinking water fleas that carry guinea worm parasites; also known as guinea worm disease

epidemiology (ep-uh-dee-mee-OL-uh-jee) *noun* the study of the patterns, causes, and control of disease in groups of people

eradicate (ih-RAD-uh-kate) *verb* to completely eliminate

exposed (ek-SPOZD) *adjective* out in the open; unprotected

extract (ek-STRAKT) *verb* to take or pull something out

filter (FIL-tur) *verb* remove materials from a liquid

flash drive (FLASH DRIVE) *noun* a small device that stores computer data

guinea worm (GIN-ee WORM) *noun* a long parasitic worm that can infect humans and other mammals in parts of Africa and Asia

host (HOHST) *noun* an animal or plant from which a parasite gets nutrition

infected (in-FEKT-ed) *adjective* invaded by a disease-causing organism

intestine (in-TEST-in) *noun* the long digestive tube extending below the stomach

larvae (LAR-vee) *noun* the immature, wingless life-forms that hatch from the eggs of many insects

larvicide (LAR-vuh-side) *noun* a chemical that kills larvae

lubricate (LOO-bruh-kate) *verb* to make something slippery or smooth by applying an oily substance to it

mate (MATE) *verb* to join together for breeding

outbreak (OUT-brake) *noun* the sudden spread of disease in a short period of time within a limited location (like a neighborhood, community, school, or hospital)

parasite (PA-ruh-site) *noun* an organism that lives on or in a host organism and causes harm to its host

pipe filter (PIPE FILL-tur) *noun* a straw-like device with a screen that is used to filter parasites from drinking water

plague (PLAYG) *verb* to cause pain and misery

prevention (pri-VEN-shuhn) *noun* the act of stopping something from happening

pus (puhs) *noun* a thick yellowish-white fluid that forms in infected tissue and contains bacteria

resource (REE-sorss) *noun* a natural source of something that people need

spleen (SPLEEN) *noun* an organ in the abdomen of humans that helps filter blood

sterile (STAIR-uhl) *adjective* unable to have children

symptom (SIMP-tuhm) *noun* a sign of an illness

tendon (TEN-duhn) *noun* a strong, thick cord or band of tissue that joins a muscle to a bone or other body part

tormenting (TOR-ment-ing) *verb* causing severe pain or suffering

water flea (WAW-tur FLEE) *noun* an organism that lives in freshwater and can be a host for parasitic worms

INDEX